WHAT'S RIGHT ABOUT WHAT'S WRONG

Poems

DONNA TRUSSELL

HELICON NINE EDITIONS
KANSAS CITY & LOS ANGELES

Copyright © 2008 by Donna Trussell

All rights reserved under International and Pan American Copyright Conventions. Published by Helicon Nine Editions, Midwest Center for the Literary Arts, Inc.
P.O.Box 22412, Kansas City, MO 64113
www.heliconnine.com

Requests to copy any part of this work should be addressed to the publisher.

Book design: Tim Barnhart

Cover photograph: Richard Ehrlich. *Namibia Sand Houses, Plate NH17*
www.ehrlichphotography.com

Acknowledgments appear on page 59.

Helicon Nine Editions, a non-profit small press, is funded in part by the National Endowment for the Arts, a federal agency; the Kansas Arts Commission and the Missouri Arts Council, state agencies, the Miller-Mellor Association; and the N.W. Dible Foundation.

MAC KANSAS
MISSOURI ARTS COUNCIL   ARTS COMMISSION

Library of Congress Cataloging-in-Publication Data

Trussell, Donna
  What's right about what's wrong : poems / Donna Trussell. -- 1st ed.
    p. cm.
  ISBN 978-1-884235-40-5 (alk. paper)
  1. Ovaries--Cancer--Patients--Poetry. 2. Cancer--Patients--Poetry. I. Title.
  PS3620.R89W47 2008
  811'.6--dc22

                                      2008023769

Manufactured in the United States of America
FIRST EDITION
HELICON NINE EDITIONS
KANSAS CITY • LOS ANGELES

WHAT'S RIGHT ABOUT WHAT'S WRONG

For Robert
Fuit Ilium

Contents

I

5	In the Gulf Stream
7	After the Lutheran Retreat
8	Hope Chest
9	Adobe Dream
10	French Movies
11	Cave of the Winds
12	A Wrong Turn Somewhere
13	Ouija
14	Pulling Weeds on a Sunday
15	Seismic Shift
16	Mythology
17	Drowning
18	This Woman
19	Radio Silence

II

23	Paris, Palo Alto, Paris
24	To Miss Candace Mayes, Lost on the *Titanic*
25	Cakewalk
26	Summer
27	Dreams, Indexed
28	Dictionary Love Affair
30	Snow
31	Promised Land
32	Thanksgiving
33	Choice
34	Julie in the Kitchen
35	Poetry: The Musical

36	Roaming at Night
37	How to Draw Locomotives
38	Nightmare at the Warehouse
39	What's Right About What's Wrong
40	Yellow Jackets
41	Dresses
42	Freedom Sickness
43	On Sky-Vue Boulevard

III

47	Skin
48	Mirror
49	Secrets of the ER
50	Letter to the Dead
51	The Oncologist and Her Ghosts
52	Premonition
53	My Daughter Undone
54	The Drunk's Wife
55	Accomplice
56	A Deeper Well
57	Madame Monet: Woman with a Parasol
58	Posthumous Poem

59	*Acknowledgments*
61	*About the Author*

I

She took her mother's car
to get away from me
Heaven knows that I,
I can sympathize
Oh I can sympathize

>from "2CV"
>Lloyd Cole and the Commotions

In the Gulf Stream

He finds her
standing alone
in the shallows,

skirt gathered
around her knees,
feet buried

in wet sand,
eyes locked
on the horizon.

Back in good
Idaho dirt, he collects
rainwater in cups.

He presses his cheek
against the well.
He dreams of her

wrapped in seaweed,
her skin yellow
lavender green.

She swims through
holes in soft
wood. Her legs

move in rhythm
to currents from below
where sunlight falls

into darkness
and eyeless fish
skate the ocean floor

driven by scent
and some dim idea
of the sea.

After the Lutheran Retreat

Of course it meant nothing,
the way he brushed against me
by the cakes and goodbyes.
His home is happy. And mine—
six years tending a garden,
smoothing a path.

We spoke only of God
as we walked to the quiet
message of stars.
My husband and children slept.
I turned my face to the trees,
so sure of themselves.

Now I shower twice a day
just to feel the water.
A cashier is rude, and I don't care.
Every morning at six
I look to see what the cat has killed
and brought in.

Hope Chest

She's the party guest
who stays too long.
The ranch dip? That's her.

She's the zoo with cages.
Means well, but a little
scary, a little cruel.

She's the trailer
with *History of Civilization*
stashed under the couch.

She wanders the cement
fog of Sartre
and her own dull manifesto.

But sometimes she hears
this whisper: O Mystery!
O Romance! O Wild West!

Kurosawa, Fellini, Ford—
she brings them her wedding
dress, her hope chest.

She joins them standing
in canyons, wading fountains
at midnight, toasting

the farmer who spends
his days with too much rain
or not enough.

Adobe Dream

A man or woman—
who can say in the shadows
of the café?

A bird flashes
across the white sky.
We drink tequila,

feel the heat rise.
Our eyes rest
on soft edges of adobe.

Children jump and run.
Toys clatter.
The sun sets.

Hours: Open
till closed.
The bartender tells

his life story
in this lush silvery
place. Moonlight

spills on the table.
We lift our glasses.
Then the night,

the man, the café
dissolve
into my flat, thin day.

French Movies

Crumbling white houses,
cats, attics,
cream and fresh parsley,
a translucent blue dress.

No one speaks in a rage
or a whisper.
I'm pregnant, she says,
calm as a nun.

Cave of the Winds

The tour guide greets
the man who comes alone.
Let's wait, she says,

someone else might come.
She's young, the sheen
of girlhood still on her face.

He sits beneath a catalpa
tree. What did a neighbor
say about catalpas?

They drop things—a dirty
tree. The plate-sized leaves
flutter like sails.

No one shows up.
The girl tightens a shoelace
and says, Let's go.

The cave walls glisten
where summer air
marries the moist

atmosphere inside.
The man can see
tiny lights on the trail.

He stops. She looks back.
Something wrong?
Yes, he says. Something.

A Wrong Turn Somewhere

They pass house after house
but none calls out.
A blue haze covers the road.

She thought she knew the way.
The road narrows to wooden
planks over a stream.

He drives on, unsure
what measure of danger
says: Go back.

Ouija

Glum, she walks
home from school.
I stretch myself thin

and lie down on the street
to feel the weight of cars
to feel what she feels.

I appear as a crack
in the sidewalk
with a ladybug and a bright

dime. She stops.
Then she sees horseapples—
round, green and sticky.

Again she trespasses
the backyards
she once named.

She'd promised
to stay out
but she can't help herself.

She settles under a willow
canopy where leaves
whisper a soft tale

of things brighter
than dimes, of a life
fuller than this.

Pulling Weeds on a Sunday

She runs her fingers
through short grass,
like her ancestors
who thrived where bears,
tigers and other hungry
beasts could not hide.

Atheists have conceded
God exists
as a pulse in the brain.
Theft is efficient.
War is natural. Rape
refreshes the gene pool.

But still she digs the earth
for tears she rationed,
prayers she silenced,
love she put back.
In dry sand even a mirage
can give you peace.

Seismic Shift

a found poem

Cats take their kittens
and hang them in bushes.
Horses refuse
to go into barns.
Fish lose their fear
of being caught.
Whales beach
themselves. They travel
magnetic
lines and suddenly
a continent
gets in their way.

Mythology

My book of mythology
had women in long flowing
robes relaxing on riverbanks.
Swans pulled sea chariots
that fit just one young
man. No chain, no anchor
not even a rail to keep him
from slipping overboard.
The chariot reins were flower
garlands. Every scene
was rich with trees,
fruit hanging low, and tame
birds alighting on shoulders.

But the gods got mad.

A man flies and his wings
melt. He plummets to earth.
Boys turn into wild boars.
A woman falls in love.
She must sort waist-high
piles of beans and grains.
Her hands press her cheeks
in surprise and dismay.
As a child I wondered
how those grains got mixed up
in the first place. Then one day
I knew: The gods did it
deliberately. Just to punish.
I was older by then.

Drowning

Planning is over.
Promises are over.
Making amends, writing
back, being clever

are finally forever over.
Think what it means
to say to your accountant:
It doesn't matter.

To the man who fixes
foundations: Oh never mind.
To the dentist:
Just give me some pills.

Then feel the warm water
envelop you.
The earth holds dear
such muddy, silty talk.

And so do you.
For this you've only
been waiting
all your life.

This Woman

These extra pounds aren't me,
this tired dress,
these vinyl shoes.
I'm not this woman
walking into this house.

> I'm the undeveloped film
> found in the basement.
> I'm the secret pocket in jeans

No one knows.
My children fight over grapes.
My husband sets his watch.

> I change colors.
> Tonight I'm turquoise
> seeping into midnight blue.

Radio Silence

He remembers her
once or twice a year,
whenever he sees
olive-skinned women
with hair to the waist.
He shakes his head
and recalls the dark girl
who almost ruined his life.

In her house he sleeps
with the dust mites.
He vibrates the floorboards
wherever she walks.
She hears him on the radio.
Between stations he hisses
with the death rattle
of distant stars.

II

"Wagon Train's a really cool show,
but did you ever notice that they never
get anywhere? They just keep on
Wagon Train-ing."

    from *Stand By Me* (1986)

Paris, Palo Alto, Paris

I live next door to an artist.
His paints are dusty.
He prefers to play chess.
My queen falls to his knight.
I won, he says, but you played
more beautifully, more
courageously. His bed smells
of sweet tobacco. Every step
we take along the Seine,
another tulip blooms.

I live with my husband
and children. They shape my days,
a basket weaving itself.
My son swaggers, then hugs
the shore. My daughter's bee sting
pierces me. I watch TV
or read Chekhov
beneath the purple, impossible
wisteria. Our long grass
ripples like silk.

I live behind the soup factory.
It's paradise back here.
I got my mailbox nailed to a tree.
I got a good man from Mexico.
My only complaint: I need
new glasses. I can't see
deep enough. I can't quite
make it out, but I can hear
chanting, when it's late,
when stars burn the sky.

To Miss Candace Mayes, Lost on the *Titanic*

You'd be gone by now anyway.
You would have married,
grated nutmeg,
buried a husband in Boston,
knitted and traveled
until your children buried you.

Instead, you clung to a winch
until the deck grew steep.
The water, icy and dark,
touched your feet. You took a deep breath.
All beings have an end, you thought.
This is mine.

For seventeen years Mrs. David Wilkins
lit a candle for you,
remembering your words:
"You go first.
You have children waiting at home."
Collapsible D, the last boat, lowered away.

Mrs. Wilkins later divorced
and went to an asylum.
She'd tried everything—
painting, charity work, a pilot's license.
Her hands would climb the trellis.
Her feet were never still.

Cakewalk

Guppies for sale
at the Little Flower Academy.
Ring toss
embroidery hoops skid.
Crepe paper brushes my cheek.

The wind kicks up.
The tetherball bumps the pole
at the cakewalk—
sixteen squares
marked on the blacktop.
The music stops
like a heart.
        Mama begged Daddy.
        I heard her tiny scared voice.

Lady in the blue dress
smiles at me.
Lipstick and pearls.
Mama is home, sleeping,
sleeping. Daddy is gone.
I am all there is.
I fit my feet
perfect on the square.

Summer

There goes pi
there goes potassium
there go products of Iowa,
facts that once mattered
now just fluttering
paper birds.

Dreams, Indexed
a found poem

Dreams of: architectural impossibilities, 57, 92, 121
of arriving at work in dressing gown, 89
of being told that Duke does not know one's surname, 121
of bull turning into a swan, 88
of card index in disarray, 137
of carrying analyst inside testicles, 80-82
of coins jammed in telephone, 81-82
of falling into machinery, 15, 101
of finding book containing truth, 124
of grating skin over salad, 81
of guest taking over kitchen, 95
of ink spots on suit, 89-90
of installing electricity, 92
of Iona Cathedral, 125
of joining exclusive club for visitors only, 124
of moon falling out of sky, 122
of nipples covered with squid ink, 81-82
of penises popping out of low-cut dress, 90
of sexual relations with detached female organ, 112
of ship bearing down on swimmer, 17
of sicknesses transformed into roses, 129
of swinging a cat, 75
of taking house to pieces brick by brick, 95
of word Earnest, 40

Dictionary Love Affair

The dictionary does not equivocate
or excuse. Or retreat.
In the dictionary you find no rebuttal,
no bargaining, no hedging.
Instead it's: Take *that*.
Put *that* in your pipe and smoke it.

Ennui: *Listless dissatisfaction
arising from a lack
of occupation or excitement.*
Dictionary, you make it sound like fun.
You make it sound continental.
Is there a non-stop to Ennui?

I did not know the word
solipsism: *The view that the self
is all that can be known to exist.*
My extended adolescence
transformed into philosophy.
Thank you Dictionary!

I fell in love with ubiquitous.
To think there's a word
for franchises, for subscription
cards that fall promiscuously
to the pavement.
For mistakes. For regrets.

A former friend introduced me
to the French word
stair thought: *As you descend
the stairs leaving a party,
the thought of what you should have said
an hour ago.*

My friend, you could say

our time together was a stair
thought in progress.
You could say my whole
life has been a stair thought.
And the stairs just keep going down.

I once encountered a sign
extolling the richness
of language. The Japanese
have a word for: *The emotion
triggered by the sight of someone
once loved, but loved no more.*

The word razbluito
did not sound Japanese
to me. That's because
razbluito is not in fact Japanese.
Razbluito is missing from every
dictionary on the planet.

Razbluito is urban legend.
I found out right after I coined
a word for: *The emotion
triggered by the sight of someone
consumed with razbluito
about you.*

Snow

She packs her suitcase—
mad red socks
and tough denim.

He doesn't touch her.
He folds his arms,
leans against the wall.

People change, he says,
I don't know why.
He walks away.

She returns her suitcase
to the spiders
and dust. Night

brings broken sleep
and cliffs dissolving
under her shoes.

She combs her hair.
Her hands
are rubber gloves.

Three days she eats
nothing.
Help me, she whispers.

He turns away.
She's seen that face before.
It's the face

he gave the man downstairs
whose car was stuck
in the snow.

Promised Land

You didn't torch a house
or sell drugs.
You had the bad luck
to be born to our family
and so you took your place
at Promised Land Home for Girls.
There you wrote letters
that disappeared
and raised a pony
that was sold.

You found comfort
in Bible stories, in hymns
of suffering and release.
You sang to God the Father
who surely donned a robe
and mounted a throne
just to hear the soft
soprano voice
of the blond girl
with the deep red heart.

Thanksgiving

One niece is dark, like me.
The other fair like—I'm told—
her father. Her radiant nature
reminds me of no one.

One niece studies bones.
The other niece can choose:
Which Explorer Would You Be
and Why, or Electricity Today.

The girls have secret notebooks:
One wants a blue Mustang.
The other wants a car made of metal
bound by magnetic field.

One writes poetry: Grandma,
I love you. You are like a rose petal.
Sister, I love you.
You are like a rodeo clown.

That's not poetry, she says,
that's just something I wrote.
She kicks the garden.
Everything is dead, she says.

Then: I don't see why
we always have to live in homes
and institutions and stuff.
I don't think we're that bad.

You're right, I say, and fall silent.
Soon enough they'll encounter
the ugly, unswerving
language of courts and lawyers.

The girls have learned
how to harmonize. They sing
softly as the sun begins to set
on the pines of East Texas.

Choice

Potatoes were a delicacy
in my mother's house
along with canned
corn and, in a rare
gourmet moment, LeSeur
young peas in their tiny
silver can. Ah,
that's what *those* people
eat. My first date dazzled
me with choice
of sour cream, chives
and bacon on my baked
potato. My my!
This is how *those* people
live. He went back to them,
of course, and there were no more
dates. Just my mother
and her back-burner
skillet of grease, my cousin
laying plans for a future
in food stamps, my brother
bringing boxes of Cap'n Crunch
to potlucks, and me
and my secret stash
of silver wrappers
and Gain-Wate wafers
that tasted like chalk
so I don't know who was gaining
weight with them.
And, oh, the occasional potato.

Julie in the Kitchen

Your husband must complain—
all that cold air
allowed to escape
while you make up your mind.
He's right, of course,
but I love the way
you just stand there,
I love the way the ghostly
light washes over your face.

Poetry: The Musical

I hate to embody
a postmodern cliché
but I must confess: I can't finish
poems. As for poems
already completed,
I won't stand in their way.
If they can emerge from quicksand
on their own, good for them.
But I'm done.

Poems are trivial.
No one reads them unless coerced.
And why should they?
We don't listen
when people ramble
about their dreams, their losing
battles. We want to kill
the neighbor who's just explaining
his philosophy,

or telling the story
of her one true love,
the one she'll never get over
the one who invented a secret
unspoken language.
Oh, you know what she means
but you don't dare tell
your wife, your husband
or anyone.

Roaming at Night

Our hands are full
of our dark writer deeds
and other pursuits.
We ride Harleys
and rusted cars that let in
the crisp October night
empty of shoppers
and bouncers. Even watchmen
have gone to sleep.
We wear jackets and black caps.
We make no greeting.
We stare without looking—
he's one of us,
she's one of us.

How to Draw Locomotives

a found poem

Your object
is to draw locomotives
and make them look
right.

Drawing wheels
is important to the successful
execution of locomotive
drawings.

Well-trained
eyes are useful
for many more things than just
drawing locomotives.

Nightmare at the Warehouse

The man says I can't leave
until I buy
something, anything.

I stroll past barrels
made into chairs, Early American
with all its little knobs

and sofas in rust,
mustard, and a brown
not found in nature.

Plaster matadors
look down as play pits
swallow whole families

and spit out shoes
like watermelon seeds.
I run for the exit

and barely miss the swing
of a swag lamp
seeking revenge on its maker.

What's Right About What's Wrong

The day you left
I tripped on the porch
and broke seven eggs.
The yolks spread
over concrete,
through dust and twigs
down to the potted yucca
that grows to one side.
Someday it will tip over.

Digging rotten bulbs
doesn't help.
You're in the soil.
I guess God loves
the two-headed calf,
the equation that solves
to an infinite fraction
that *can't* be right,
but is.

Yellow Jackets

My wife wonders
why nothing works.
Four times I've called.
Four times the man
has bombed, fogged, sprayed.

I keep telling him:
They built the nest
inside the walls.
Why should I have to tell him?
It's his business, not mine.

I work hard. I don't cheat.
If my wife cries
it's onion or ammonia.
We live well.
The baby changed nothing.

We swat till my wife
collapses. I shout
and growl. Still
the yellow jackets come,
late at night

they crawl from the baseboard.
At dawn they're beneath
my wife's feet
as she steps from the shower.
And on me, while I sleep.

Dresses

My closet is full. Dress
after dress—faded, limp,
stained, stretched, torn.

Or too bold. My slut
dress caused many problems.
Hard to wash too.

The lacy prom dress
I got married in. My velvet
Mardi Gras robe.

Most are just too young—
cherries on green background,
hobbyhorses on blue,

hot pink cotton
with white spaghetti straps,
sandals worn down to nothing.

I always forget their flaws.
I always believe
in their redemption.

Freedom Sickness

The vice cop
began turning tricks.
She's lost her mind, they said.

Or was it the freedom
sickness? The sick can afford
anything—

their families, their jobs,
even their lives.
Imagine the young blue-eyed

lawyer who flies to Iraq
to found freedom centers.
She dies of course.

Did freedom drive her crazy?
Or does sickness make freedom
irresistible?

The teacher seduces a child.
She goes to jail.
Now they're married.

The cancer patient
leaves her annuals
to the frost. She can't bear

to crush them as trash.
Imagine red petals
blooming in snow.

Imagine nature
unraveling
to let her in.

On Sky-Vue Boulevard

We lived next to a thrift shop.
We bought grinning
ceramic peaches,
a twenty-dollar bed,
an old book:
The Chinese Way of Love.

You quit both your jobs.
I quit one of mine.
No one complained.
We slept with the windows
open then. If a recipe
called for three, I put in four.
My bread was wet
and never done, remember?

Now I measure carefully,
and every night you walk
from window to window,
making sure they're locked.

III.

Out of a misty dream
Our path emerges for a while,
Then closes within a dream

        from "Vitae Summa Brevis"
        Ernest Dowson, 1867-1900

Skin

My ghost stopped by
while touring her former life.
I was taking a bath,
my legs stretched out
my feet on white tiles,
a bruise on my shin
next to the scar
I seared twenty years ago
smoking hash
in a red room somewhere.

My ghost had a scar too
only hers was faded.
Everything was faded
except the look of longing
on her face. She said
she'd forgotten
what it was like to have skin
so tangible and pink,
what it was like
to have a future to decide.

Mirror

In front of the mirror I tried
to imagine my young brown eyes
and Dutch-boy haircut
on a woman older than my mother.
I could not see that woman.
Perhaps, I thought, I will die young.

But I grew up. And I met you.
Our pre-war building had wide
hallways and big windows—
breezeways from another time.
To us that still mattered. Just the idea
of air flowing free mattered.

Our building was bulldozed
long ago, but the park is still there.
We had a view! I'd forgotten
the Red Canna, the strong sun,
the private shady walks.
We must have felt like kings.

Nearby was a diner called
China Clipper, with a shiny
airplane in front.
It took so little to make us happy.
Even my terrible job was good
because I could leave.

We knew nothing of trouble
then. Just awkwardness.
Just superstition. What I would give
to be a misfit, a degenerate, a confused
wild girl. What I would give
to see her in the mirror again.

Secrets of the ER

One day you're whipsawed
with anguish,
and red-faced regrets,

and the next you're flat
on your back,
taking in your pristine

new surroundings—
the cool rooms, the clear
plastic tubing

and the calm faces
of those who try and try
to reverse gravity.

At first you go along.
At first you believe
in their magic.

But someday you'll turn
away from white
walls and good intentions.

Someday you'll recall
your sanguine self
and you'll say:

I miss you.
Come back.
All is forgiven.

Letter to the Dead

I speak to you
from the fragile net of the living.

I know you.
I've walked with you.

My grandmother,
to whom I could give

not one drop
of my youth, my health.

Soldiers, proud
and scared.

A girl in a car
submerged.

She looked so shocked.
I would be shocked too

had I not already
walked with you.

The Oncologist and Her Ghosts

Her nightmares are blizzards—
words swallowed by wind,
and faces frozen
beneath ice and snow.

She wakes with a start.
She rises, lies down, comforts
herself with memories
of another time

before cities, before textbooks
before patients who smiled
and joked and died.
No matter what she did, they died.

She recalls a night
on her father's farm.
Southern gusts swayed
the moon-tipped trees.

Above her were the only
gods she knew. She made a pact:
The stars would protect her
and she would save lives.

She was just a child then,
and even in Nebraska
summer seemed endless
and full of promise.

Premonition

She drops her dishtowel.
What was that?
A possum? A neighbor?

Houdini, back at last?
An idea blooms in her mind
like a black tulip:

She will die falling.
Her past will play out
floor by floor, much too fast.

One dog, two cats,
her mother's red kiss,
a pink eraser

from her father.
The dress she loved
because it was reversible.

She must get ready.
She gives everything away—
money, books, her lover,

new plates
still in the box.
But there's always more.

She envies babies
with just smiles
and soft skin.

She envies the Sphinx,
with only wind
and sand.

My Daughter Undone

Not a single cell.
She was just an idea,
a morning vapor
gone by noon.
My womb disappeared
with the sweep
of a surgeon's knife.

I would apologize
but she can't believe it's over.
I thought she'd fade
but still she calls
in the sleepless night:
give me your darkest winter
it will be spring to me

The Drunk's Wife

Her aquarium still glows
and pumps. The hum
fills the room,
a stand-in for sounds
she can't hear—
glass dripping
threads stretching
dust sifting down.

Every day she walks by
and expects to see
her betta fish,
blue with a red tail
like a Japanese fan.
Then she remembers:
He died. He turned
lavender and died

headfirst in a plant
with long supple leaves
that gave him more
comfort than she did
with her tapping,
her yearning to see him
swim again
or even shudder.

Accomplice

With you I go where
rain falls up,
walls are porous
and night's black ribbon
folds back on itself.

I plummet.
I'm no one, nothing.
You've made me
an accomplice
in my own demise.

A Deeper Well

My husband's pallbearers
have thick, pink faces
and the luxury of grief.
I can't make a sound.

The house gels around me.
I get up, I go looking
at the white shoes of spring.
Choose ten. Buy none.

Wine digs a deeper
well, but I drink
and fold into the waxleaf
bushes of last summer,

a trip we did not take,
instead lounging
in the evening air
with a day-for-night moon

and wind strong enough
to drown out the howling
coyotes and the cries
of their prey.

Madame Monet:
Woman with a Parasol

You are 28 and you know
nothing of illness now
as you stand in tall grass and yellow

wildflowers. Behind you
a brilliant blue sky, white clouds
and your young son.

Your skirt swirls
as though you suddenly turned
to face the artist

casting a shadow at your feet.
Did he say something?
Or did you hear

someone say: Don't move.
Cancer will soon engulf you.
Stay in that meadow. I will join you.

Posthumous Poem

You're busy
and I'm no star
no statesman
no young girl in hiding.
I'm not famous
or even almost famous,
and so you're not there.
You're not reading this poem
that self-destructs.
Still, I have to ask:
Who are you?
What do you do?
Tell me, is the sun out?

Acknowledgments

The author wishes to thank David Baker, Kelly Barth, Rick Bass, Michelle Boisseau, Barbara Bolz, Bread Loaf Writers Conference, Margaret Broucek, Susan Cahill, Noreen Cargill, Kacey Carlson, Raymond Carver, Kay Cattarulla, G.S. Sharat Chandra, Michael Collier, Dallas Museum of Art, Jim Daniels, Stephen Dunn, Mary Eaton, John Mark Eberhart, Sherri Eberhart, Carla Eskelsen, Reginald Gibbons, Dana Gioia, Paul Haenel, Susan Hahn, Melinda Henneberger, T.R. Hummer, Yaedi Ignatow, Dan Jaffe, Gretchen Johnsen, Felicia Knight, Jo McDougall, James McKinley, Patricia Cleary Miller, Philip Miller, Catherine Browder Morris, Rebekah Presson Mosby, *Newsweek*, Naomi Shihab Nye, Tim O'Brien, Karl Patten, Rick Peabody, Pembroke Hill & Youth Poetry Symposium, Robert Pinsky, Michael Pritchett, Shannon Ravenel, C.L. Rawlins, David Ray, Judy Ray, Trish Reeves, Jan Schall, Christine Shields, Ann Slegman, Sharon Sheehe Stark, Robert Stewart, Robert Love Taylor, Patricia Traxler, *TriQuarterly*, Gloria Vando, Vermont Studio Center, Maryfrances Wagner, Zoe Walrond, Norman Wendth, Susan Whitmore, The Writers Place, and the other writers, teachers, editors and friends who lit the way.

Some of the poems in this book were previously published, sometimes in different form, in the following magazines and anthologies:

Best of Northlight, "Nightmare at the Warehouse"
*Chance of a Ghost (*Helicon Nine Editions): "The Oncologist and
 Her Ghosts"
Chicago Review: "Radio Silence"
Confrontation: "Adobe Dreams"
Descant: "How to Draw Locomotives"
Forum: "On Sky-Vue Boulevard"
I Feel a Little Jumpy Around You (Simon & Schuster): "Snow" and
 "This Woman"
Is This Forever Or What? (Greenwillow)*:* "Radio Silence"
*Kansas City Outloud II (*BkMk Press): "A Deeper Well,"
 "Snow," and "To Miss Candace Mayes, Lost on the Titanic"

*Living in Storms (*Eastern Washington University Press): "Snow"

The Massachusetts Review: "Paris, Palo Alto, Paris"

New Letters: "Dreams, Indexed"

Oyez Review: "French Movies"

The Plum Review: "After the Lutheran Retreat"

Poetry: "To Miss Candace Mayes, Lost on the *Titanic*" and
      "On Sky-Vue Boulevard"

Poetry Kanto: "In the Gulf Stream" and "What's Right About What's Wrong"

Poetry Northwest: "Snow" and "Cakewalk"

Poets at Large (Helicon Nine Editions): "In the Gulf Stream" and
      "Paris, Palo Alto, Paris"

The Quarterly: "This Woman"

Spud Songs (Helicon Nine Editions): "Choice"

Tar River Poetry: "A Deeper Well"

Texas Observor: "Letter to the Dead"

West Branch: "Roaming at Night"

About the Author

Donna Trussell grew up in Texas. Today she lives in Kansas City with her husband. Her poetry and fiction have appeared in *Poetry, TriQuarterly, North American Review,* and other journals. In the past she has worked as an editor, film critic, and teacher.

Her short story "Fishbone" appeared in *Fiction of the Eighties, New Stories From the South, Growing Up Female,* and other anthologies. "Fishbone" was nominated for the Pushcart Prize, was a finalist for *Best American Short Stories* and was performed as a play in Seattle and as a monologue in Dallas. "Fishbone" can be found online at www.donnatrussell.com and in the SMU Press book *Texas Bound II.*

In 2001 Trussell was diagnosed with ovarian cancer. Five years later *Newsweek* published her essay "Remember Me as a Writer, Not a Survivor."